PUFFIN BOOKS

The Bee's Knees

Roger McGough is one of Britain's most popular poets. He has been captivating children and adults alike with his unique blend of compassion and wit for more than three decades and with more than thirty books. He is an international ambassador for poetry and was awarded an OBE for his work in 1997. In 2001 he was honoured with the Freedom of the City of Liverpool.

The Bee's Knees

ROGER McGough

illustrated by Helen Stephens

PUFFIN

For Francesca and Daniele Nasi

PUFFIN BOOKS

Published by the Penguin Group
Penguin Books Ltd, 80 Strand, London WC2R 0RL, England
Penguin Putnam Inc., 375 Hudson Street, New York, New York 10014, USA
Penguin Books Australia Ltd, 250 Camberwell Road, Camberwell, Victoria 3124, Australia
Penguin Books Canada Ltd, 10 Alcorn Avenue, Toronto, Ontario, Canada M4V 3B2
Penguin Books India (P) Ltd, 11 Community Centre, Panchsheel Park, New Delhi – 110 017, India
Penguin Books (NZ) Ltd, Cnr Rosedale and Airborne Roads, Albany, Auckland, New Zealand
Penguin Books (South Africa) (Pty) Ltd, 24 Sturdee Avenue, Rosebank 2196, South Africa

Penguin Books Ltd, Registered Offices: 80 Strand, London WC2R 0RL, England

www.penguin.com

First published 2003
1

Text copyright © Roger McGough, 2003
Illustrations copyright © Helen Stephens, 2003
All rights reserved

The moral right of the author and illustrator has been asserted

Set in Goudy & Clubhouse

Made and printed in England by Clays Ltd, St Ives plc

British Library Cataloguing in Publication Data
A CIP catalogue record for this book is available from the British Library

ISBN 0-141-31495-8

Contents

The Opening Poem   1

Puppy Cat   2

Dog Talk   4

Imagine If ...   6

The Girl Who Became a Book   8

Tommy Doesn't-Care   13

How to Make it Stop Raining   14

Imaginary Friend   16

I'd be a Good Friend   19

Clock Watching   20

Glug   21

Ten   22

The Kitten's First Spring   24

Spelling Bees   28

Total Eclipse   30

In Here   34

Out Here   35

The Colour Collector   36

M. Barra-Sing   40

A Silly Wish   42

Cool Cat   44

Good News   46

Bee's Knees   48

Lucky Dad   50

Stop, Thief!   51

The Rolling Meatball   52

The Local Fire Brigade   54

Cos   58

Ink   58

No Room in My Room   59

The Room   60

The Opening Poem

This is the opening poem
Like the opening song of a show
Its job is to settle you down
With a smile and a cheery 'Hello!'

All the characters in the book
Are hoping you'll visit their page
So nervous and overexcited
You'd think they were going on stage.

Dancing pigs and puppy cats
Glow rats and elephants on skis
Look forward to meeting the reader
Because you're, without doubt,
    The Bee's Knees.

(Just kidding about the elephants on skis.)

Puppy Cat

I wanted a dog to call my own
One to fetch sticks and chew on a bone

To run like the wind, let loose in the park
To play on the carpet well after dark

So Dad went to town and when he
  came back
He brought home a puppy all shiny
  and black

And there she is (I think she's a she)
Though she doesn't look like a dog to me

He says that because she's a special breed
Kit-e-Kat is her favourite feed

And she needs a litter-tray out in the hall
Which doesn't sound very doggy at all

Perhaps when she's older she'll learn to
  bow-wow
For now my puppy says only mee-ow.

Dog Talk

Cow says 'Moo'
Duck says 'Quack'
Dog says 'Scrunch my ears
and ruffle my back.'

Pig says 'Oink'
Bird says 'Tweet'
Dog says 'Gimme a bowl
of biscuits and meat.'

Sheep says 'Baa'
Horse says 'Neigh'
Dog says 'Get up lazybones
let's go out and play.'

Hen says 'Cluck'
Cat says 'Miaow'
Dog says 'OK, I give in,
Woof woof, bow wow.'

Imagine If . . .

Kittens were slimy
Rabbits were prickly
Crocodiles were cuddly
Tigers were tickly!

Imagine if...

Dogs had webbed feet
Penguins had antlers
Snakes had feathers
Ducks had trunks!

Imagine if . . .

Elephants could hop
Birds could bark
Pigs could dance on one trotter
Hippos could swing from tree to tree!

Imagine how funny
the world would be!

The Girl Who Became a Book

This little girl loved books.

Her happiest times were when she was
   snuggled up in bed listening to Mummy
   or Daddy reading stories.

Stories about sad princesses
   and huge castles
      and roaring dragons
         and hungry caterpillars
           and naughty kittens.

Stories about buffaloes on bicycles
kangaroos and koala bears
hippos and penguins
chocolate ice-creams
and sweet sweet dreams.

"When I'm three and a half," she said,
"I want to be a book."

And she thought about it so hard
and she wanted it so much
that one night her wish came true!

There she was in bed next morning:
  the sweetest book imaginable.

At first, Mummy and Daddy missed having
  their little girl around the house.
Meal-times were too quiet
  and bath-times were no fun any more.

But they soon got used to the idea.

Whenever they took her out in her push-chair
people would stop, pick her up, and read a
few words.

In the park, she was always the centre of
attention.

One morning, in the local bookshop,
she got lost!
Oh dear, what if somebody else buys her?
But Daddy found her just in time.

At last
(and perhaps because of the nasty scare
in the bookshop)
the little girl changed her mind about
being a book.
She had grown tired of sleeping on the
bookshelf.
And lonely too,
for books are quiet and tend to keep to
themselves.

She decided that she wanted to be a
child again.

And so she became one.

Tommy Doesn't-Care

Little Tommy Doesn't-Care
Scruffy jeans
Untidy hair
Gets into fights
Uses both feet
What Tommy says
Goes in our street

Little Tommy Doesn't-Care
There's no one tough or meaner
Especially if you should dare
To call her Thomasina!

How to Make it Stop Raining

Drawing, drawing
Is boring, boring.
I'd rather be out
But it's pouring, pouring.

I'm stuck here alone
With paper and crayons
Squiggling and wriggling
For aeons and aeons.

I'm losing my temper
(That's nothing new)
I'll throw a tantrum
And then throw a shoe.

Or … I could make a picture
And colour it blue
Add red for anger
With black patches too.

Wrap my bad mood in it
And throw it away
To make it stop raining
So I can go out and play.

Imaginary Friend

I've got a friend
no one can see
That nobody hears
only me

He's not a ghost
or anything scary
A cartoon rabbit
or a wicked fairy

He's hard to describe
(looks a bit like me)
Though bigger and stronger
like I want to be

He's there each morning
and throughout the day
We watch telly together
read or play

There are jokes to tell
and secrets to share
When I'm not well
it's good that he's there

We seldom argue
we never fight
(Because I'm the one
who's always right)

I know he's not real
it's only pretend
And I'll grow out of him
in the end

For when I'm older
I intend
To find an
un-imaginary friend.

I'd be a Good Friend

Everyone's a friend of someone
Although it seems to be
That every friend has got a friend
Who's not a friend of me.

I'd be a good friend to someone
Fun to be with, and kind.
I'd be as happy as an eight-armed goalie
As sweet as a jam roly-poly
As cool as a knickerbocker glory
As warm as a bedtime story
If only a friend I could find.

Clock Watching

The church clock stands at ten to eleven
The grandfather clock sits at half past three
The alarm clock jumps at five to seven
The stopwatch stops and watches me.

Glug

My name is Doug
I'm a garden slug
Snug inside this empty jug.

Oh dear, it's raining ...
Glug, glug, glug ...

21

Ten

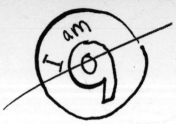

I'm 10! I'm 10!
I'll never be 9 again

I used to be 5
And I used to be 4

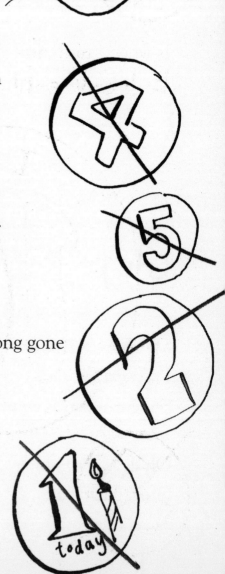

And I'll never be 2
Or 3 any more

I used to be 1
But those days are long gone

I'm 10! I'm 10!
Not 6, 8 or 7

And the only time
I'll stop being 10

Is when I turn into
E-l-e-v-e-n!

I am
10

23

The Kitten's First Spring

There's a robin
There's a bluebird
Tail a'bobbin
It's a new bird

There's a crocus
Puts in focus
My first spring.

There's a March hare
What a sprinter
Been in training
All through winter

Pussy willow
What a thrill, O
My first spring.

A day-old foal
Legs a jumble
Like he's on stilts
Takes a tumble

He shakes his mane
Then tries again
His first spring.

See the hedgerow
Smell the blossom
When the wind blows
It'll toss 'em

While daffodils
Embrace the hills
My first spring.

Count the cowslips
Hear the bluebells
All the colours
All the new smells

Just a daisy
Can amaze me
My first spring.

Spelling Bees

In the hive at the bottom
of the garden live 26 bees

I have named each one
after a letter of the alphabet

A swarm is unreadable
but when they land on flowers to refuel
or settle on grass to sunbathe
they spell out words like these:

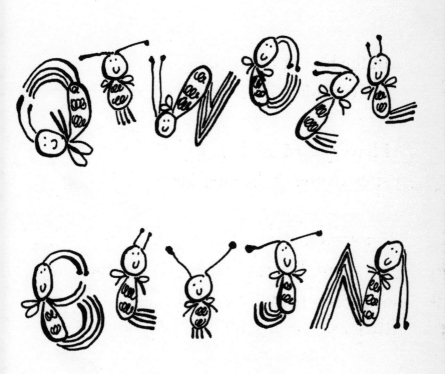

It's a difficult language
the language of bees.

Total Eclipse

the oxen are flummoxed

wildebeest bewildered

baboons bamboozled

turtles startled

geese aghast

cats catatonic

sharks shocked

terrapins terrified

rattlesnakes rattled

spiders in a spin

tigers in a tizzy

for 45 seconds,
as long as it took
for the moon
to blot out the sun

In Here

I used to be a cloud
  but now I'm an ankle
I used to be a leaf
  but now I'm a finger
I used to be a raindrop
  but now I'm an eyelash
I used to be a breeze
  but now I'm a voice
I used to be a sunrise
  but now I'm a heartbeat
I used to be out there
  but now I'm in here

     And I like it.

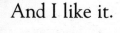

Out Here

I used to be an ankle
　　but now I'm a cloud
I used to be a finger
　　but now I'm a leaf
I used to be an eyelash
　　but now I'm a raindrop
I used to be a voice
　　but now I'm a breeze
I used to be a heartbeat
　　but now I'm a sunrise
I used to be in there
　　but now I'm out here
　　　　　　I'm the universe!

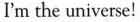

The Colour Collector

A stranger called this morning
Dressed all in black and grey
Put every colour into a bag
And carried them away

The goldenness of cornflakes
The ivory of milk
The silverness of soupspoons
The see-throughness of silk

The greenness of tennis-courts
When play has just begun
The orangeness of oranges
Glowing in the sun

The blueness of a dolphin
Nosing through the sea
The redness of a robin
Breasting in the tree

The creaminess of polar bears
Sliding on the floes
The little piggy pinkness
Of tiny, tickly toes

The sky that smiled a rainbow
Now wears a leaden frown
Who's sobbing in his caravan?
Wizzo the monochrome clown

A stranger called this morning
He didn't leave his name
We live now in the shadows
Life will never be the same.

M. Barra-Sing

Sir asks a question
you really should know
You give the wrong answer
three times in a row
Who's the one who points the finger?
M. Barra-Sing

Texting coolly
down the street
You drop your mobile
at your feet
Who's the one who starts the laughter?
M. Barra-Sing

The deejay plays
your favourite track
You get up to dance
fall flat on your back
Who's the one you'd like to strangle?
M. Barra-Sing

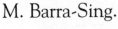

Who makes you blush
from ear to ear?
Who makes you want
to disappear?
Who's to blame for everything?
M. Barra-Sing.

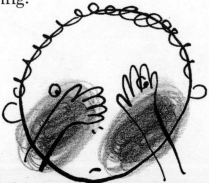

A Silly Wish

Admiring fire-flies
darting to and fro,
a young rat thought
'If only I could glow
like that.'

Its wish came true.

Now each night
it hides inside
the garden shed
as owls circle overhead
attracted by the light.

'A silly wish,'
the glow-rat said,
with hindsight.

Cool Cat

My cat may look like your cat
With know-it-all eyes like yours
Spreadeagling itself on your tummy
To practise sharpening its claws

My cat may look like your cat
With sticky-out whiskers like yours
And the knack of slipping off branches
To land safely each time on all-paws

My cat may sound like your cat
With a pitiful mew like yours
After scratching the arms of the sofa
Tries to burrow under closed doors

My cat may look like your cat
And my cat may sound like yours
But my cat plays the saxophone
And dances to wild applause.

Good News

Here are the clues:

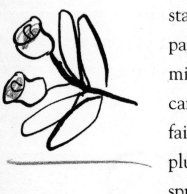

starry pies
paper nights
mince hats
carol lights
fairy singers
plum holly
sprigs of snow
mistlebells
sleightoe
duff crackers

Here is the news:

It's Christmas!

Bee's Knees

Ever seen a bee slip?
Ever kissed a bee's lip?

Ever felt a bee slap?
Ever sat on a bee's lap?

Ever made a bee start?
Ever eaten bee's tart?
   (rose petals and honey)

Ever told a bee 'Stop'!
Ever spun a bee's top?

Ever heard a bee sneeze?
Ever tickled bee's knees?

Nor me.

Lucky Dad

I am her bee's knees
Her Easter egg
Her name on gifts
under Christmas trees
Her lucky bag.

I am her solemn promise
Her fingers crossed
Her prayer to Saint Anthony
when things get lost
Her lucky dad.

Stop, Thief!

There's something about the seaside
I don't understand

Who steals the footprints
We leave in the sand?

The Rolling Meatball

I was eating spaghetti
It tasted just great
When one of the meatballs
Jumped off the plate

Before I could ask
My mother for more
It rolled through the kitchen
And out of the door

I tried to catch it
But I tried in vain
It rolled down the road
Fell into a drain

I rang the police
And the fire-brigade
Who arrived with a net
A rope and a spade

They scooped it out
(It was covered in slime)
'Thanks,' I cried
And without wasting time

Hurried back home
Where the meatball, of course
I ate with a dollop
Of tomato sauce.

The Local Fire Brigade

Help! Help! Help!

If your house has caught alight
In the middle of the night
Pick up a phone, call nine-nine-nine
We'll put it out in double quick time

Cos we're the local fire brigade
We're quickly on the scene
We wear big hats and welly boots
And keep our hoses clean

Help! Help! Help!

If your kitten's up a tree
Miaow, miaow, catastrophe
Pick up a phone, call nine-nine-nine
We'll rescue puss in double quick time

Cos we're the local fire brigade
No emergency too small
We wear big hats and welly boots
And answer every call

Help! Help! Help!

If little Jimmy's head is stuck
In the railings, you're in luck
Pick up a phone, call nine-nine-nine
We'll chop it off in double quick time

… Only joking

Cos we're the local fire brigade
We answer every call
We wear big hats and welly boots
Except at the Fireman's Ball

Help! Help! Help!

If your dog has gone astray
Not been seen since yesterday
Pick up a phone,
    call canine-nine-nine
We'll bring him home in double quick time

Cos we're the local fire brigade
And when it's suppertime
Our mums and wives will let us know
By calling nine-nine-nine.

Cos

Our hamster loved lettuce
So we called him Cos
But sadly he died
Before he knew who he was.

Ink

In dusty classroom cupboards
bottles of ink
spend years on end
wondering what they did wrong.

No Room in My Room

My room is very, very small
The bed is up against the wall
Ceiling too low to toss a ball

Whenever Grandad pays a call
(Although he's old, he's very tall)
On bony knees he has to crawl

The smile on the cat says it all:
No room to swing me, room's too small.

The Room

Hello! Thanks for calling
I'm just off on my bike
That's my room up there
Take a look if you like.

I'm Norman the door
I'm always on guard
Monsters, vampires
And grown-ups are barred.

But I will admit
I've got more than one side
So if you wipe your feet
I'll open up wide.

Hi! I'm Sybil the sofa
I've got room for you all
Stretched out and comfy
The length of the wall.

I'm Charles the chair
And I'm made out of wood
And I stand up straight
Like a proper chair should.

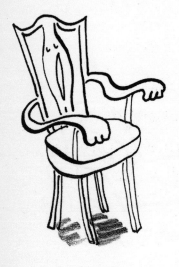

Not like that Sybil
What a right lazy lump!
Found I don't doubt
On a garbage dump.

Or taken from a skip
On a dark, dark night.
If I had my way
She'd be set alight.

Did you hear what he said?
What a horrid old stick.
If he wasn't antique
I'd give him a kick.

I feel sorry for him
If the truth were known
He was born one of six
Now he's all on his own.

Excuse me! Excuse me!
Won't you look where you're walking!
You'll miss the best part
If you're too busy talking.

I'm Kismet the carpet
Handwoven on a loom
By artists in India.
Aren't I Queen of the Room?

Hi! I'm Doug the rug.
(Keep the place snug.)

I'm Miranda the mirror
Do you like what you see?
Typical! People look at themselves
Hardly ever at ME.

I'm Winston the window
Got a smile on my face
When I let the sunshine
Stream into the place.

And I'm Kirsten the curtain
I'm usually quite prim
Though I'm terribly proud
To hang out with him.

I swish and I glide
Hanging on to the rail
But when the wind blows through Winston
... I billow like a sail.

As you've guessed, I'm a desk
I'm called Mister Trevor.
Ink-stained and wrinkled
I'm terribly clever.

(Unlike the BOY
I have to report
Who only likes music
And TV and sport).

I'm Nelly the telly
Yes I'm his best friend
He just sits and stares
For hours on end.

He laughs at my jokes
To my music he dances
When I ask any questions
He shouts out the answers.

I'm Bessie the bed
Sorry about the mess.
Who plays football in his sleep?
Go on. Have a guess.

I'm Larry the lamp
And the reason I'm bright
Is that I sleep through the day
And most of the night.

Take my advice
And get plenty of rest
So when you're switched on
You can shine at your best.

I'm Philip the fireplace
Does my tummy roll!
What wouldn't I give
For a nice lump of coal.

Four regiments of books
Too numerous to mention
Ready for action
We stand to attention.

My name is a number
A brand new PC
And since I arrived
He's had eyes just for me.

I'm Timmy the toy box
I hold all the treasure
That over the years
Has given such pleasure ...

Lego, Transformers,
A guitar without strings,
Cars, rubber dinosaurs,
An elephant with wings.

Glove puppets, a skateboard,
Marbles, and rings,
Seashells and pebbles
All magical things.

Quiet everybody!
Somebody coming!

Hello, I'm back.

What do you think of my room?

Boring, isn't it?

the end